SKILLS JOURNAL

¿Amazing English!™

AN INTEGRATED ESL CURRICULUM

Michael Walker

Addison-Wesley Publishing Company

ISBN 0-201-85374-4
3 4 5 6 7 8 9 10-CRS-99 98 97

CONTENTS

A Publication of the World Language Division

Director of Product Development: Judith M. Bittinger
Executive Editor: Elinor Chamas
Content Development: Kathleen M. Smith
Editorial Development: Elly Schottman
Text and Cover Design: Taurins Design Associates
Art Direction and Production: Taurins Design Associates
Production and Manufacturing: James W. Gibbons

Illustrators: Teresa Anderko 44, 63, 64; Dolores Bego 59; Mena Dolobowsky 40, 50, 57, 83, 96, 101, 106, 107; Nancy Didion 43; Franklin Hammond 6, 7, 12, 25, 84; Linda Knox 26, 106; Susan Lexa 66, 95; Susan Miller 5, 8, 13, 62, 78, 85, 99, 102, 103; Diane Palmisciano 86; Chris Reed 9, 18, 27, 30, 32, 43, 48, 49, 60, 68, 83, 90, 98, 109; Karen Schmidt 108; Jackie Snider 11, 14, 24, 42, 61, 87.

Quick Writes

Write and illustrate some sentences about your friends. What are their names? Where are they from? Where do they live now? What do you like to do together?

_____

_____

_____

_____

_____

_____

_____

_____

_____

_____

(Supports Student Book C, page 3) **Freewriting on unit theme.** After discussing friends, students write about the topic. You may want to save this page in the student's **Assessment Portfolio.**

A *Interview five friends. Fill in the chart. Compare your chart with your classmates' charts.*

Person Interviewed	Best Friend's Name	Age	Older or Younger Than Me	What We Like to Do Together

Fill in the crossword puzzle.

Across

3. Is your best friend a _____ or a girl?
6. What's your _____ ?
4. Maria is my best _____ friend.
8. Is she _____ or younger than you?
9. My friend's_____ name is Rosita.

Down

1. Is your friend older or _____ than you?
2. What do you like to do _____?
5. What _____ you like to do best?
7. My friend's _____ name is Perez.

(Supports Student Book C, page 4) **Data collection; interviewing; asking for and recording information; completing a crossword puzzle.** Tell students to write *Older* or *Younger* in column 4 of the first exercise. Students use the completed chart as springboards for more paired conversations to practice. You may want to save this page in the student's **Assessment Portfolio**. Correct the second exercise in class.

*True or False? Look at the pictures. Read the sentences. Write **True** or **False** on the lines.*

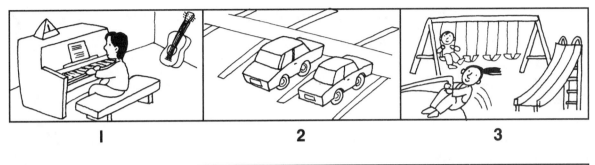

1   2   3

4   5   6

1. A boy is in the music room. He is playing the piano. _____

2. Two cars are in the parking lot. _____

3. There are three swings on the playground. _____

4. A girl is sleeping in the cafeteria. _____

5. Two boys are playing basketball in the gym. _____

6. A teacher is reading in the library. _____

Rewrite the false sentences to make them true.

_____

_____

_____

(Supports Student Book C, page 5) **Comparing written language with pictures; rewriting false statements as true.** Correct in class.

Weekend Fun

A. *Write some sentences about what you do on the weekend. Do you play with your friends? Do you visit relatives? Do you help your family?*

(Supports Student Book C, page 7) **Home-School Connection; creative writing based on a song.** Students write about weekend activities. Hold a discussion/give more prompts as necessary to students who need extra prewriting stimulation. Allow time for students to read their paragraphs aloud to the class. You may want to save a copy of this page in the student's **Assessment Portfolio**. Have students take this page home to share with their families.

COMMUNICATION 2

A Make sure you know these numbers.

first	1st	tenth	10th	twenty-first	21st
second	2nd	eleventh	11th	twenty-second	22nd
third	3rd	twelfth	12th	twenty-third	23rd
fourth	4th	thirteenth	13th	twenty-fourth	24th
fifth	5th	fourteenth	14th	twenty-fifth	25th
sixth	6th	fifteenth	15th	twenty-sixth	26th
seventh	7th	sixteenth	16th	twenty-seventh	27th
eighth	8th	twentieth	20th	thirtieth	30th
ninth	9th			thirty-first	31st

Look at the calendars. Correct the sentences on a separate piece of paper.

1. The first Thursday in June is the tenth.

2. The second Monday in July is the fifteenth.

3. The third Friday in May is the fourth.

4. The first Wednesday in June is the twentieth.

5. The second Tuesday in May is the third.

6. The third Saturday in July is the twelfth.

(Supports Student Book C, page 8) **Vocabulary development: ordinal numbers; reading a calendar.** Review the numbers in the list with students. Correct the second exercise in class.

A Ask ten people, "What day were you born on?" For each answer, draw a birthday cake next to the day of the week. You will make a bar graph. The first one is done for you.

Sunday	
Monday	
Tuesday	
Wednesday	
Thursday	
Friday	
Saturday	

The most students were born on _____.

The fewest students were born on _____.

(Supports Student Book C, page 8) **Data collection; interviewing; graphing.** Completion of the interview questions will result in a bar graph; students may need to ask at home which day they were born on.

B *Unscramble the names of the months.*

1. lipra   5. bcteroo
2. rebpesmet   6. ruanajy
3. yma   7. cahmr
4. atugsu   8. yujl

Which months are missing from the list? _____ ,

_____ , _____ , and _____

Unscramble the names of the days of the week.

1. sedweaydn   4. nudays
2. dyaastru   5. daysuste
3. ruradthsy   6. ridyfa

Which day is missing? _____

Write the name of each item.

1. _____

4. _____

2. _____

5. _____

3. _____

6. _____

© Addison-Wesley Publishing Company

(Supports Student Book C, page 9) **Vocabulary development: days, months, common items.** Students should be able to complete this page independently. Pair more able students, who will finish first, with weaker students, who may need extra help. You may want to save this page in the student's **Assessment Portfolio**.

Check This Out!

A. *Write a new poem. Use the words in the Data Bank or any words you want!*

I'll be your friend
For as long as you like

I'll share all my _____
                1

I'll lend you my bike

We'll go to the _____
               2

We'll play in the park
I'll hold your hand tightly
When we walk in the dark

I'll hug you _____
              3

If you ever cry
And I'll give you half

Of my _____ pie
        4

Together we'll be

_____ we'll be
     5

Very _____ friends
        6

Just you and me

DATA BANK

1. toys
   tapes
   baseball cards
	3. tight
	   close
	   twice
		5. Forever
		   Always
		   Together

2. mall
   museum
   game
	4. cherry
	   apple
	   chocolate
		6. closest
		   nicest
		   best

B. *Interview three friends. Ask them, "What makes a good friend?"*
Fill in the chart. Compare your chart with your classmates' charts.

Person Interviewed	Answer
1.	
2.	
3.	

(Supports Student Book C, pages 10-11) **Cloze poetry; interviewing.** Encourage free choice of words for the completion of the poem and praise all efforts. Volunteers can read their poems aloud. In Exercise B, students interview three classmates and complete the chart. Allow time for students to share their information.

More About Alligators and Crocodiles

C. *Read the paragraph and answer the questions.*

Alligators and crocodiles are big reptiles. They live in rivers and lakes in warm parts of the world. They have few natural enemies. Some adult alligators and crocodiles can grow as big as 20 feet long. They eat fish and other animals, like birds and frogs. As they grow older, they sometimes look for bigger animals to eat.

1. A snake is a reptile. What other reptiles do you know about?

_____

2. Do crocodiles and alligators usually live on land, in the sea, or somewhere else?

_____

3. Some adult humans can grow as tall as 6 or 7 feet. How long can an alligator or crocodile grow?

_____

4. What do crocodiles and alligators eat?

_____

5. Do young animals eat the same things as older animals?

_____

6. Find out one more fact about crocodiles and alligators.

_____

(Supports Student Book C, page 11) **Reading for a purpose; writing; research.** Correct numbers 1–5 in class. Suggest appropriate reference materials for number 6 and have students share their facts. You may want to save this page in the student's **Assessment Portfolio**.

A Answer with **Yes, I do**, or **No, I don't**.

1. Do you like to dance? _____.

2. Do you like to draw? _____.

3. Do you like to sing? _____.

4. Do you like animals? _____.

5. Do you like fruit? _____.

6. Do you like vegetables? _____.

Draw your favorite animal, vegetable, and fruit.

12

(Supports Student Book C, page 12) **Expressing likes and dislikes; writing; art.** Students use familiar vocabulary to express likes and dislikes of various items. Encourage oral presentations of the students' own art. Some students may be able to label their art, or you may label for them.

B *Write the time for each clock or watch.*

1. 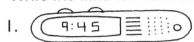 9:45

2.  8:30

3.

_____ _____ _____

4.

5.  2:45

6.  4:30

_____ _____ _____

Use the pictures and the words to write conversations like the one on page 13 of your student book. The first sentence one is done for you.

Let's go to the football game on Saturday.

1. Saturday / 2:00

_____

_____

_____

2. Friday / 3:30

_____

_____

_____

3. Saturday / 10:00

_____

_____

_____

(Supports Student Book C, page 13) **Telling time; writing conversations.** Students complete both exercises independently. Allow students to work with their student books open, if necessary. You may want to save this page in the student's **Assessment Portfolio**.

A. *Use a ruler to measure some things in your classroom. Then fill in the last two items.*

    1. book

    _____

    2. eraser

    _____

    3. _____

       _____

    4. _____

       _____

B. *Weigh some things in your classroom. Use the scale you made on page 15 of your student book. Then fill in the last two items.*

    1. bookmark

    _____

    2. stapler

    _____

    3._____

       _____

    4. _____

       _____

C. *Read each sentence. Write **True** or **False** on the lines.*

An elephant is heavier than a cat. <u>True</u>

1. My pencil is heavier than my eraser. _____

2. My English book is heavier than my math book. _____

3. My shoe is heavier than my chair. _____

4. My chair is heavier then my desk. _____

5. My ruler is heavier than my pen. _____

(Supports Student Book C, pages 14-15) **Measuring and weighing; mathematics; recording information.** Students can work independently or with a partner for Exercises A and B. Correct Exercise C in class.

A New Friend Named Charlie

Write a letter to a family member who lives far away.
Here are some ideas to write about:

your new town	your new friend
your new school	your new sport
your new home	your new uniform

_____

(month and day)

Dear _____

_____

_____

_____

_____

_____

_____

_____

Love,

_____

(Supports Student Book C, pages 16-17) **Home-School connection; letter writing.** Hold a brainstorming session, using questions about students' activities in class, at home, and in sports. Volunteers can share their letters. Students can copy them to send if they want to. You may want to save a copy of this page in the student's **Assessment Portfolio**. Have students take this page home to share with their families.

Soccer Facts

Read the paragraphs and answer the questions.

There are eleven players on a soccer team. Players try to score goals. You score a goal if you kick or head the ball into the goal. The goalkeeper tries to stop the ball from going into the goal. The goalkeeper is the only player who can stop the ball with his or her hands. The goalkeeper is also the only player who is allowed to pick up the ball.

A soccer game lasts for ninety minutes. After forty-five minutes, the players take a rest. This is called half-time. Then they play for another forty-five minutes.

The most important soccer competition is called the World Cup. Teams from almost every country in the world play in the World Cup.

1. How many players are there on a soccer team?

_____

2. Who can pick up the ball?

_____

3. How can you score a goal?

_____

4. How long does a game last?

_____

5. What is **half-time**?

_____

(Supports Student Book C, pages 16-17) **Reading for a purpose; writing.** Check answers in class.

Let's Play Soccer

Complete the sentences.

First, you need _____ teams of _____ people. Each team tries to

get the _____ across the _____ to the opposite _____. To

score a _____ , you must _____ the ball past the _____
and into the net.

The _____ is the only player who can touch the ball with his or her

_____ when it's in play. Other players use their _____ ,

_____ , _____ , or _____ to hit the ball.

To _____ is to kick the ball while running.

To _____ is to use your feet to take the ball away from an _____ .

To _____ is to kick or nudge the ball to your team _____ .

To _____ is to pretend to kick or pass, and then do

something _____ .

To _____ is to break a rule.

Open your student book to pages 18 and 19. Check your answers.
You get two points for every correct answer. Correct any wrong
answers or spelling.

YOUR SCORE:_____

(Supports Student Book C, pages 18-19) **Vocabulary development; cloze exercise.** Before students begin
this page, reread aloud, or play the tape of, the student book pages so students can hear the information
again. Then have them work independently. You may want to save this page in the student's **Assessment
Portfolio**.

American Football

Read the paragraphs and answer the questions.

American football is not like soccer. Most people in the world call soccer "football," but in America, football is a different game. A soccer ball is round. An American football is oval, like an egg. Soccer teams have eleven players. American football teams have forty players, but only eleven players are on the field at one time.

In American football, you score a touchdown if you catch the ball in the end zone or carry it there. Players can catch the ball with their hands. They can run with it and throw it to other players. You can tackle a player even if the player does not have the ball. All this is against the rules in soccer.

Each year, the top two football teams play in the Superbowl. This final game is like the world championship in American football.

1. What is the difference between a football and a soccer ball?

_____

2. How many players are there on a football team?

_____

3. What can you do in American football that is not allowed in soccer?

_____

4. How can you score a touchdown in football?

_____

5. What is the Superbowl?

_____

(Supports Student Book C, pages 18-19) **Reading for a purpose; writing.** Check answers in class.

Dorothy and Her Friends

*Use the words in the Data Bank. Finish the paragraphs about
"Dorothy and Her Friends."*

Dorothy lived in _____. One day, a _____ carried her

house far, far up in the _____. Her house finally landed in the Land of

_____. It also landed right on the Wicked Witch of the _____!

Strange little people called _____ greeted Dorothy. _____

_____, the Good Witch of the North, was _____ there.

"_____ ! We are so grateful. You have _____ the Wicked

Witch of the East," said the Good Witch.

"Oh no, there must be _____ mistake," said Dorothy. "I have not
killed anything."

"Your house did, anyway. See? These are her _____!"

"But where am I?"

"In the Land of Oz, of course."

"Oh. Can you help me find my way _____ to Kansas?"

The Munchkins and the Good Witch told Dorothy to ask the Wizard of Oz for

_____. The Wizard lived in Emerald City.

DATA BANK

toes	Oz	Kansas
Their	killed	East
Munchkins	help	cyclone
some	back	friend
also	Welcome	sky

(Supports Student Book C, page 20) **Reading comprehension; cloze exercise; syntax.** Students read sentences from the story they listened to on student page 20. This exercise provides an opportunity for students to review the story and to learn syntax. Correct in class. You may want to save this page in the student's **Assessment Portfolio.**

Make an Amazing Facts game of your own. Use facts from this book and your student book. You can write new facts, too. Write the correct answers on a separate piece of paper. Ask your teacher to check your game before you exchange games and play with friends.

(Supports Student Book C, page 22) **Creating a game; reading and writing; socializing.** Some students may need help, especially for this first game. Encourage students to research answers they don't know. Store games in a box students can access during free time.

Quick Writes

Write and illustrate some sentences about your family. Do you have brothers or sisters? What are their names? Are they older or younger than you? Do you have grandparents? Aunts and uncles? Write about them. What things does your family like to do together?

_____

_____

_____

_____

_____

_____

_____

_____

_____

_____

© Addison-Wesley Publishing Company

(Supports Student Book C, page 23) **Home-School connection; freewriting on unit theme.** After discussing families, students write about the topic. You may want to save a copy of this page in the student's **Assessment Portfolio**. Have students take this page home to share with their families.

A Interview five friends. Fill in the chart. Compare your chart with your classmates' charts.

Person Interviewed	Family Size	Brothers/Names	Sisters/Names	Pet
1.				
2.				
3.				
4.				
5.				

Write questions for these answers.

1. _____

   My family is small.

2. _____

   I have no brothers.

3. _____

   I have two sisters.

4. _____

   Their names are Maria and Theresa.

5. _____

   Maria is eight and Theresa is four.

6. _____

   Yes, I do. I have a rabbit.

(Supports Student Book C, page 24) **Data collection; interviewing; asking for and recording information.** Students use completed charts in the first exercise and questions and answers in the second exercise as springboards for more paired conversations to practice. You may want to save this page in the student's **Assessment Portfolio.**

Label the rooms of the house.

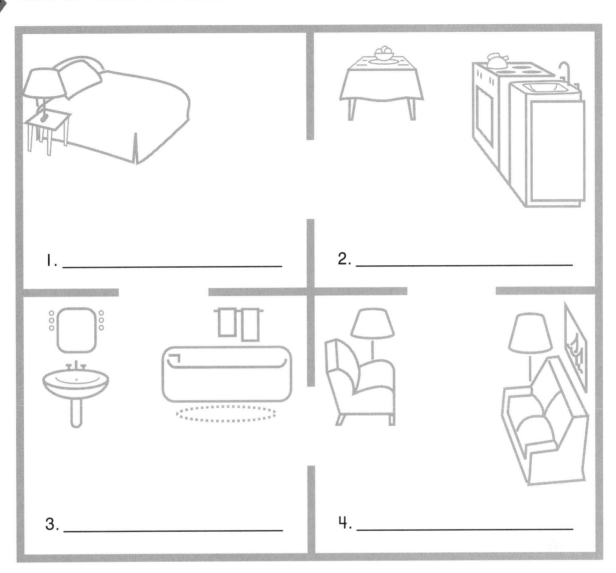

1. _____

2. _____

3. _____

4. _____

Draw somebody in your family in each room. Tell what each person is doing.

1. _____

2. _____

3. _____

4. _____

(Supports Student Book C, page 25) **Home-School Connection; vocabulary development.** Students complete the page independently. Help students self-check word order and spelling in the second exercise. Encourage students to tell you more about their drawings to further evaluate vocabulary acquisition and oral production. Have students take this page home to share with their families.

Food Chains and Food Webs

Read the paragraphs and answer the questions.

Many animals eat grass. Other animals eat the grass-eaters. Then other animals eat the animal-eaters. A simple food chain can go like this:

Grass.　　A rabbit eats the grass.　　A fox eats the rabbit.

or like this:

Grass.　　A cow eats the grass.　　A human eats the cow.

Green plants make their own food from water, soil, and sunlight. Animals spend a lot of time looking for food. They eat plants. They get energy from plants.

Many food chains together make a web. All living things are linked in food webs. So you can see why a change in the number of plants or animals can make a big difference to all the animals in the world.

1. How do green plants get food?

_____

2. Why do some animals eat grass and plants?

_____

3. Explain what a food chain is.

_____

4. Explain what a food web is.

_____

5. Why are food webs important?

(Supports Student Book C, page 26) **Reading for a purpose; writing.** Check answers in class. You may want to save this page in the student's **Assessment Portfolio**.

My Family

Make poems about your family. Here is an example.

My ___uncle___ was born

In the year of the ___fish___.

So he likes to ___swim___.

1. My _____ was born

   In the year of the _____.

   So _____ likes to _____.

2. My _____ was born

   In the year of the _____.

   So _____ likes to _____.

3. My _____ was born

   In the year of the _____.

   So _____ likes to _____.

4. My _____ was born

   In the year of the _____.

   So _____ likes to _____.

(Supports Student Book C, page 27) **Home-School connection; cloze poetry.** Encourage free choice of words for the completion of the poem and praise all efforts. Volunteers can read their poems aloud. Have students take this page home to share with their families.

A

1

2

3

4

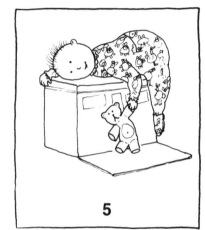
5

6

Tell where the baby is. Use complete sentences.

1. _____

2. _____

3. _____

4. _____

5. _____

6. _____

(Supports Student Book C, page 28) **Describing locations with prepositions of place.** Students describe the pictures, using prepositions of place. Follow-up: students practice asking *where* questions referring to the baby on the page or to objects that they have placed around the classroom: *Where's my English book? It's under your desk.*

B Complete the crossword puzzle. Use the clues below and the Data Bank on page 29 of your student book.

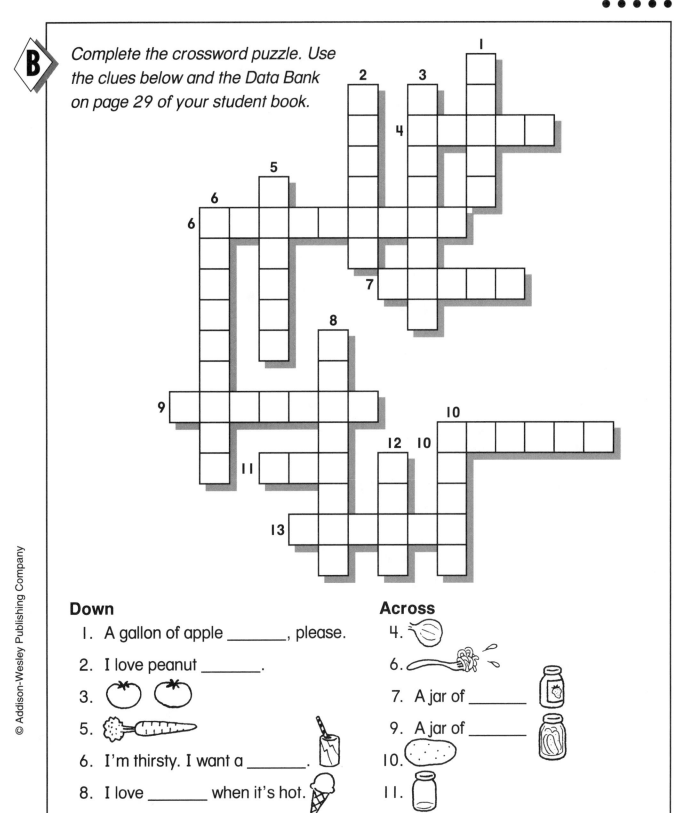

Down

1. A gallon of apple _____, please.

2. I love peanut _____.

3. [tomatoes image]

5. [carrot image]

6. I'm thirsty. I want a _____. [drink image]

8. I love _____ when it's hot. [ice cream image]

10. A _____ of onions, please.

12. We get _____ from cows.

Across

4. [onion image]

6. [spaghetti on fork image]

7. A jar of _____ [jam jar image]

9. A jar of _____ [pickle jar image]

10. [potato image]

11. [jar image]

13. A _____ of milk

(Supports Student Book C, page 29) **Completing a crossword puzzle; food vocabulary.** Students work independently. Correct in class. You may want to save this page in the student's **Assessment Portfolio**.

27

A. *Complete the sentences.*

1. You will eat _____ peanut butter sandwiches by age _____ .

25,000	13
1,500	18
15,000	38

2. The busiest day for the phone company is _____ .

    Christmas
    Father's Day
    Mother's Day

3. More than 103 _____ people call a _____ on that day.

thousand	Dad
million	Father
hundred	Mom

B. *Many people speak English all over the world. But English is not exactly the same in every country. We all understand each other, but sometimes we use different words.*

British English	**American English**
autumn	fall
lift	elevator
pavement	sidewalk
petrol	gas
tap	faucet
toilet	restroom or bathroom

If a British person says this, what does an American say? Write complete sentences on a separate piece of paper.

1. Don't walk in the street. Walk on the pavement.

2. I have to stop for petrol.

3. Take the lift to the tenth floor.

4. She is coming home in the autumn.

5. The tap in the toilet is broken.

(Supports Student Book C, pages 30-31) **Reading for a purpose; appreciating cultural differences in language.** Correct Exercise A in class. Students can complete exercise B independently or in pairs.

C. *Listen carefully and complete the sentences. Then open your student book to page 31 to check your answers.*

Did you know that ants live in "families" called _____? The colonies can

be big, with many thousands of _____. The colonies can be small, with

only a _____ ants. Ant homes can be under the _____, in

_____, or in high mounds.

Ants are _____ insects. That means they live and work together. There

is a _____ ant for every colony of worker ants. Some ants have

_____ and some don't.

Ants aren't very friendly to ants in other colonies They make _____ on

smaller ants. They drive the smaller ants out of their _____ and

_____ their eggs. When the eggs hatch, they make the new ants work as

_____ in their colony.

Driver ants are really _____. Driver ants live in parts of _____

and Asia. Even the biggest and the strongest animals are afraid of driver ants.

These ants march in long _____ , like an army, and attack _____ in

their way. Any animals in the ants' way will be covered with millions of _____!

One way to fight off an attack is to find water and _____ the driver ants.

(Supports Student Book C, page 31) **Cloze exercise; listening.** Read aloud the article on student book page 31 as students listen only. Read again and pause as students fill in the blanks. You may want to save this page in the student's **Assessment Portfolio**.

A. *Label the food.*

1.

_____

2.

_____

3.

_____

4.

_____

5.

_____

6.

_____

B. *Read the paragraphs and answer the questions.*

   You eat food for energy to keep fit and healthy. Your muscles use energy when you move. Your brain needs energy when you think. You get energy from carbohydrates and fat in your food.

   You also get proteins, vitamins, and minerals in your food. These help to repair damaged body parts and give you healthy blood and strong bones.

   People in different countries grow and eat different foods. Rice is the main food for more than half the people in the world. But too many people in the world do not get enough to eat.

1. When do your muscles need energy?

_____

2. Why are carbohydrates and fat important?

_____

3. Why are vitamins and minerals important?

_____

4. What do more than half the people in the world eat?

_____

(Supports Student Book C, page 32) **Food vocabulary; reading for a purpose; writing.** Students complete the page independently. Correct in class. You may want to save this page in the student's **Assessment Portfolio**.

A. *Unscramble the sentences to make conversations.*

1. brothers many does have she how

_____

two has she brothers

_____

2. have does sisters many how she

_____

she one sister has

_____

3. do they many how pets have

_____

have six they cats

_____

B. *Answer the questions about your family on a separate piece of paper.*

1. How many brothers do you have?

2. How many sisters do you have?

3. Do you have a pet?

4. How many aunts do you have?

5. How many uncles do you have?

6. How many cousins do you have?

(Supports Student Book C, page 33) **Home-School Connection; family vocabulary; asking/answering questions about families.** As students re-order the sentences in Exercise A, help them with capitalization and punctuation. You can set up Exercise B to have pairs of students interview each other. Have students take this page home to share with their families.

A. *Unscramble the words that tell where your bones are.*
   Label the picture.

   1. kenc _____
   2. risfegn
   3. mra _____
   4. etso
   5. ehad _____
   6. nhda _____
   7. neke _____
   8. dlsrhoeu _____
   9. tfoo
   10. gle _____
   11. wbleo

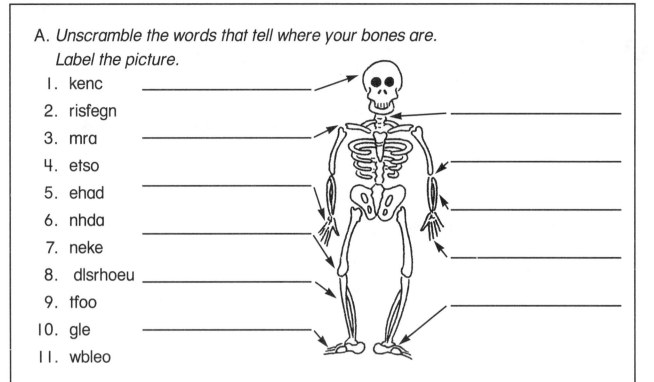

B. *Read the paragraphs and answer the questions on a separate*
   piece of paper.

   Bones are not dead. They are alive. That is why they can
mend and grow again if you break them. Some bones are as
strong as steel, but steel is much heavier.

   Bone marrow is inside many bones. Blood runs through the bone
marrow.

   In the beginning, a baby's bones are very soft. They are made
of cartilage. The tip of your nose and your ears are made of
cartilage.

   The longest bone in your body is your thigh bone. It goes from
your hip to your knee. Take care of it!

1. Why can bones mend after you break them?

2. Are bones heavier than steel?

3. Which "bones" in your body are soft?

4. Which is the longest bone in your body?

(Supports Student Book C, page 34) **Body parts vocabulary; reading for a purpose; writing.** Check answers
in class. You may want to save this page in the student's **Assessment Portfolio.**

The Squeaky Door

Complete the sentences.

1. Sonny liked to visit his _____ house in the daytime.

2. But he didn't like to spend the _____. Sonny was really scared

   of a _____.

3. The door began to squeak, and Sonny _____ right out of bed.

4. Grandma came running and said, "You can _____ with the cat."

5. Sonny was scared again when the _____ squeaked.

6. Grandma came running and said, "You can sleep with the cat and the

   _____."

7. Then the _____ door scared Sonny and the cat and the dog.

8. Grandma came running and said, "You can sleep with the cat and the dog

   and the _____."

9. Soon the _____, the _____, the _____ , and Sonny heard

   a squeak and jumped out of bed!

10. Grandma came running and said, "You can sleep with the cat and the dog

    and the rooster and the _____."

(Supports Student Book C, pages 36–41) **Cloze exercise; retelling a story in sequence; vocabulary development; reading for a purpose.** After students complete the page independently, they can work with a partner: one reads the sentences aloud and the other fills in the missing words. Encourage the students to finish telling the story orally. You may want to save this page in the student's **Assessment Portfolio.**

The Squeaky Door

Answer the questions in complete sentences.

1. What country is Sonny from?

_____

2. When does Sonny love to visit his Grandma?

_____

3. What is Sonny afraid of?

_____

4. Does he go to bed by himself or does his Grandma tuck him in?

_____

5. Does the kitchen door or the bedroom door begin to squeak?

_____

6. What does Sonny cry?

_____

7. Does Grandma or Grandpa come running?

_____

8. Which animal does Sonny sleep with first?

_____

9. What other animals does Grandma tuck in with Sonny?

_____

(Supports Student Book C, pages 36-41) **Recalling details; drawing conclusions; reading for a purpose; writing.** Students complete the page independently. Help them think of questions and answers that finish telling the story. You may want to save this page in the student's **Assessment Portfolio**.

The Squeaky Door

*Write more parts to "The Squeaky Door." Use the words in the Data
Bank or your own words. Make up a new ending.*

One night, the _____ in the _____ began to
<u>1</u> <u>2</u>

_____. Sonny _____ right out of bed and said,
<u>3</u> <u>4</u>

" _____ ." Grandma came _____ up the stairs.
<u>5</u> <u>6</u>

She said, "You can sleep with the _____ .
<u>7</u>

Then you won't be scared, will you?"
"Not me," said Sonny.

But then the _____ in the _____ began
<u>8</u> <u>9</u>

to _____. Sonny _____ into the _____.
<u>10</u> <u>11</u> <u>12</u>

Grandma came running. She said, "You can sleep with the _____ .
<u>13</u>

Then you won't be scared, will you?"

But Sonny was still scared. So _____.

_____

DATA BANK

1. windows doors	2. kitchen living room	3. squeak shake	4. jumped rolled	5. Help Grandma
6. racing running	7. cow pig	8. walls floor	9. bedroom bathroom	10. squeak rattle
11. ran raced	12. bathroom closet	13. ducks chickens		

(Supports Student Book C, pages 36-41) **Guided/creative writing; cloze story.** Students complete the page
independently. Encourage them to use their own words if they want. Volunteers can share their stories with
the class.

Bambi and the Butterfly

Use the words in the Data Bank. Finish the paragraphs about "Bambi and the Butterfly."

Bambi was a few _____ old. He loved to ask his

_____ questions. "Who does this _____ belong to?"

asked Bambi.

"To us _____," answered _____ mother.

"What are deer?" _____ asked.

"You are a deer," his mother _____. "I am a deer. We are both

deer. Do you _____?"

"Yes, I understand. I am a _____ deer, and _____

are a _____ deer!"

They came to a _____, open space. "What is it?" asked Bambi.

"It is the _____," answered his mother. The meadow was

_____ of new _____.

DATA BANK

little	meadow	you
full	days	things
his	sunny	big
understand	laughed	Bambi
mother	deer	path

(Supports Student Book C, page 42) **Reading comprehension; cloze exercise; syntax.** Students read sentences from the story they listened to on student page 42. This exercise provides an opportunity for students to review the story and to learn syntax. Correct in class. You may want to save this page in the student's **Assessment Portfolio.**

Make an Amazing Facts game of your own. Use facts from this book and your student book. You can write new facts, too. Write the correct answers on a separate piece of paper. Ask your teacher to check your game before you exchange games and play with friends.

(Supports Student Book C, page 44) **Creating a game; reading and writing; socializing.** Some students may need help. Encourage students to research answers they don't know. Store games in a box students can access during free time.

Quick Writes

What do you think of when you see this word? Write down the words
you think of. Then write a paragraph about SPACE.

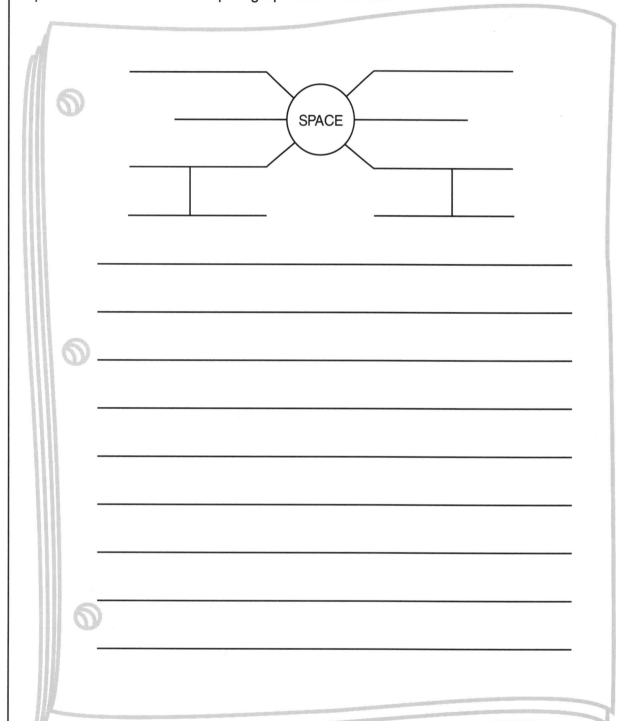

SPACE

(Supports Student Book C, page 45) **Prewriting; writing a paragraph.** After students have discussed the
illustration and titles on student book page 45, put the word *rocket* on the board. Circle it. Ask, "What do you
think of when you see this word?" Write student responses around the word *rocket*. Students do this page
independently, using their words to write a paragraph about SPACE. Volunteers can read their paragraphs to
the class. You may want to save this page in the student's **Assessment Portfolio**.

COMMUNICATION 1

A. *Interview five friends. Fill in the chart. Compare your chart with your classmates' charts.*

Person Interviewed	Favorite Hero	Favorite TV Show	Where I'd Like to Travel in Space

B. *Read the paragraphs and answer the questions on a separate piece of paper.*

More people live in China than in any other country in the world. Much of the land is desert or mountains. It is very difficult for the Chinese people to grow enough food. Many people are farmers. They grow mostly vegetables and rice.

People in China used paper, printing, compasses, and canals long before people in other parts of the world did.

For about 3,000 years, China had emperors. Just over 2,000 years ago, an emperor built the Great Wall of China to keep out foreigners.

1. How many people live in China?

2. Why is it difficult to grow enough food there?

3. What do most people eat?

4. What things did the Chinese people use before other people did?

5. When did an emperor build the Great Wall?

(Supports Student Book C, page 46) **Data collection; interviewing; asking for and recording information.**
Students use completed charts in the first exercise as springboards for more paired conversations to practice.
Correct the second exercise in class. You may want to save this page in the student's **Assessment Portfolio.**

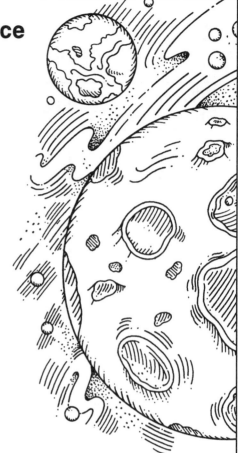

More About Space

Read the paragraphs and answer the questions.

There are nine planets around the sun. Their names are Mercury, Venus, Earth, Mars, Jupiter, Saturn, Uranus, Neptune, and Pluto. Some of these planets, like Earth, are hard balls of rock. Other planets are giant balls of gas—we think!

Jupiter is the biggest planet. It is more than 1,000 times bigger than Earth. It has at least four moons. You can see them through a telescope.

Pluto is the farthest planet from the sun. It is between 2,700 and 4,600 billion miles from the sun. You know that Earth goes around the sun once every year. Well, Pluto orbits the sun once every 248 years!

1. How many moons does Earth have?

_____

2. How many moons around Jupiter can you see through a telescope?

_____

3. Which planet is farthest from the sun?

_____

4. How often does Earth orbit the sun?

_____

5. How often does Pluto go around the sun?

_____

(Supports Student Book C, page 47) **Reading for a purpose; writing.** Make sure students understand the word *orbit.* Students complete the page independently. Check answers in class.

Exploring Space

Read the paragraphs and answer the questions.

When astronauts leave their spaceships, they must wear a spacesuit with a special helmet and gloves. The spacesuit protects them from radiation. It also gives them air, water, and power.

A space station has everything astronauts need. Of course, they must bring food, air, and water up from Earth. Astronauts can add one space station to another and build bigger and bigger stations for more and more people.

Sometimes, scientists send rockets with no people on board to explore other planets. These rockets are called probes. Probes have flown past Jupiter, Saturn, Uranus, and Neptune. The probes have sent close-up pictures back to Earth.

Communication satellites send TV, radio, and telephone signals around the world. These satellites "stand still" about 22,000 miles above Earth. Really, they do not stand still, but they move at the same speed as Earth. So it looks like the satellites are always in the same place.

1. How does a spacesuit protect an astronaut?

_____

2. What must astronauts bring from Earth up to space stations?

_____

3. How do astronauts make space stations bigger?

_____

4. What is a probe?

_____

5. Why do communication satellites seem to "stand still"?

_____

(Supports Student Book C, page 48) **Reading for a purpose; writing.** Students complete the page independently. Check answers in class. You may want to save this page in the student's **Assessment Portfolio**.

41

The Spaceship

Write and illustrate your own poem. Give your poem a title.
Use the words in the Data Bank or your own words.

_____
(title)

I dreamed I built a _____
1

Just big enough for me;

I _____ around the planets,
2
To see what I could see.

I set my course for _____
3
And zoomed around and around;

I landed on a _____ ,
4
And got some rocks from the ground.

I said hello to _____
5
And flashed around the sun;

I _____ in my spacesuit.
6
It was a lot of fun.

DATA BANK

1. rocket	2. zoomed	3. Mars
spaceship	flew	Jupiter
4. star	5. Venus	6. rested
comet	Saturn	floated

(Supports Student Book C, page 49) **Cloze poetry.** Encourage free choice of words for the completion of the poem and praise all efforts. Volunteers can read their poems aloud.

COMMUNICATION **2**

A Match each picture to a word below.

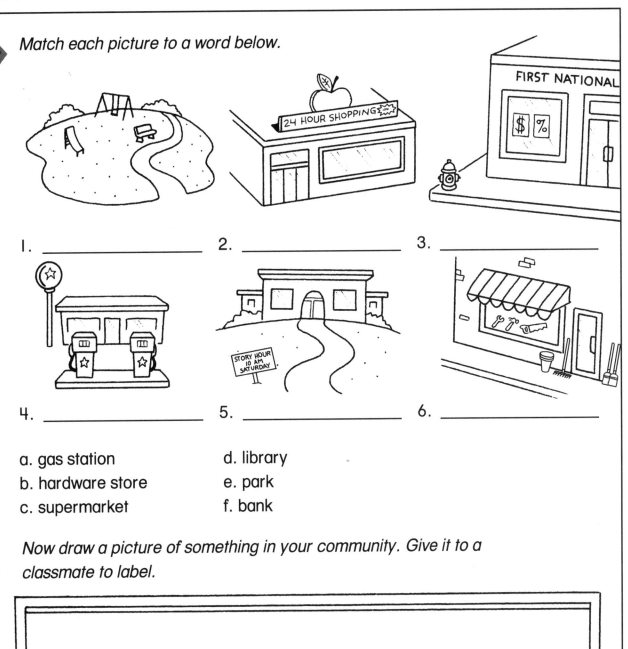

1. _____   2. _____   3. _____

4. _____   5. _____   6. _____

a. gas station
b. hardware store
c. supermarket

d. library
e. park
f. bank

Now draw a picture of something in your community. Give it to a classmate to label.

(Supports Student Book C, page 50) **Home-School Connection; matching written language to pictures.**
Students write the letter of the correct label under each picture. Brainstorm with the class about interesting places in your city or town that students may want to draw. Have students take this page home to share with their families.

43

B *What coins do they have? Color in the correct coins with a yellow crayon.*

1. Linda has 75¢.

2. Tran has 45¢.

3. Arthur has $1.00.

4. Gen has 60¢.

(Supports Student Book C, page 51) **Identifying coin values; mathematics content skills (addition).** Bring in some coins for students to work with. They need to see the real coins to understand their values. Have students work with a partner.

A. *Complete and illustrate the paragraph.*

A meteor is a chunk of _____ flying through

_____. When a meteor hits the earth, it's called a

_____. A huge meteorite hit the earth and _____

about 20 to 40 _____ years ago. Where did it land? Near what is

now Winslow, _____ . It blasted a hole, called a _____,

about 1.2 kilometers wide and 170 meters deep.

B. *Read the paragraphs and answer the questions.*

   The moon is a satellite of Earth. It is a lifeless place with no air
or water. There is no wind or any other kind of weather on the
moon. The moon takes about a month to orbit Earth. In that time,
we see its shape change. First, it is a thin crescent, then a full
moon, and then a thin crescent again.

1. Why is the moon a lifeless place?

_____

2. What does Earth have that the moon does not have?

_____

3. How long does it take for the moon to go around Earth?

_____

4. Why do you think the moon seems to change its shape?

_____

(Supports Student Book C, pages 52-53) **Reading for a purpose; writing.** Students complete the page independently. Check answers in class. You may want to save this page in the student's **Assessment Portfolio**.

45

C. *Read the paragraphs and make a model.*

The Solar System

The sun and all the things in orbit around it are called the solar system. You can make a model of the solar system to help you understand just how big it really is. All you need are ten popsicle sticks or tongue depressors. Take them to a park or playground with your friends.

Write the names of all the planets and the sun on the sticks. Push the stick with the name of the sun on it into the ground. Then, starting from the sun each time, put all the other sticks around it like this:

Mercury	half a step away
Venus	three-quarters of a step away
Earth	one big step away
Mars	one and a half steps away
Jupiter	five big steps away
Saturn	ten big steps away
Uranus	21 big steps away
Neptune	32 big steps away
Pluto	42 big steps away

D. *Write about making your model.*

_____

_____

_____

_____

_____

(Supports Student Book C, pages 52-53) **Following instructions: making a group model of the solar system; writing.** If you have an outdoor space with enough room, let a few groups of students make the solar system model and compare results. Volunteers can share their sentences in Exercise D.

LANGUAGE POWER

A Answer the questions about life on the moon.

What were you doing on the moon?

1. (drive / moon buggy)

_____

2. (build / space station)

_____

3. (collect / rocks)

_____

4. (grow / plants)

_____

Answer the questions about life on Earth.

Where are you going? What are you going to do there?

1. (library / return a book)

_____

2. (post office / mail a letter)

_____

3. (supermarket / buy groceries)

_____

4. (mall / shop for shoes)

_____

(Supports Student Book C, page 54) **Past progressive in conversations; present progressive review; space vocabulary.** Students can do these exercises independently. You may want to save this page in the student's **Assessment Portfolio**.

B *Complete the sentences.*

1. She is looking for _____ _____.

2. I am looking for _____ _____.

3. He is looking for _____ _____.

4. We are looking for _____ _____.

5. They are looking for _____ _____.

6. You are looking for _____ _____.

7. It is looking for_____ _____.

Answer the questions. Use page 55 of your student book.

Example:

The dog is looking for its bone. Where is the bone?

<u>   It's next to the basket.   </u>

1. They are looking for their shoes. Where are they?

_____

2. He is looking for his bat. Where is it?

_____

3. She is looking for her skate. Where is it?

_____

4. They are looking for their sweaters. Where are they?

_____

(Supports Student Book C, page 55) **Reviewing subject pronouns, possessives, and progressives.** Students can do these exercises independently.

The Amazing Ice Age

Read the paragraphs and answer the questions.

Long ago, ice covered many parts of the world. It was cold for a very long time. The land was frozen and the seas were full of ice.

Scientists believe that the marks on rocks in the Sahara Desert come from huge, moving sheets of ice during the Ice Ages.

The latest Ice Age began about 1,800,000 years ago. It ended about 11,000 years ago. The Ice Age lasted a very long time!

Many animals had to move from their homes to find a warmer place to live. Some had to change their eating habits and find new food. Others died out altogether.

1. When did the last Ice Age begin?

_____

2. When did the last Ice Age end?

_____

3. What did scientists find in the Sahara Desert?

_____

4. What happened in the Ice Ages?

_____

5. Why did animals have to find new homes?

_____

(Supports Student Book C, pages 56-57) **Reading for a purpose; writing.** Students complete the page independently. Check answers in class. As an extension, you can have students locate the Sahara Desert on a map and find out some facts about it.

Natural Energy

Read the paragraphs and answer the questions.

Almost all the energy we use comes from the sun. The energy is stored in the food we eat and in the coal, oil, and gas we burn.

Green plants use the energy from the sun to make their food from water and gases in the air. We eat the plants and get our energy. Or we eat animals that eat plants.

We need energy even when we are asleep to keep us warm. We also need energy to move our muscles.

Millions of years ago, plants and animals took energy from the sun as they grew. When they died, they turned into coal, oil, and natural gas.

Scientists tell us that the sun has enough energy to keep it shining for another 5,000 million years!

1. Where does our energy come from?

_____

2. How do green plants use energy?

_____

3. Where does coal come from?

_____

4. Why are coal, oil, and natural gas full of energy?

_____

5. Will the sun die soon?

_____

(Supports Student Book C, pages 56-57) **Reading for a purpose; writing.** Students complete the page independently. Check answers in class.

Tip Top Adventures

Complete the "Tip Top Adventure."

1. Tip and Top _____ a planet covered with water.

2. They put their_____ in orbit just above the water.

3. They _____ their space submarine.

4. Splash! They _____ into the water.

5. They _____ strange fish and plants.

6. The octopus _____ the sub with its eight arms.

7. Top _____ a button.

8. Eight boxing gloves _____ the octopus out.

9. The octopus _____ them through the water.

10. Top _____ for the surface.

11. The sub _____ into the air.

12. Tip and Top _____ onto the spaceship's ladder.

It was another close call!

(Supports Student Book C, pages 58-59) **Reading for a purpose; cloze story.** Students complete the page independently. Check answers in class. You may want to save this page in the student's **Assessment Portfolio**.

Tip Top Adventures

Complete the crossword puzzle.

Tip and Top _____ (2) a _____ (1) _____ (3) with water.

They put their _____ (4) in orbit just above the water.

They _____ (7) out their space _____ (11).

Splash! They dove into the water.

They saw _____ (6) fish and plants.

Suddenly, Top saw a _____ (13), hairy space _____ (5).

It lifted the sub with its eight _____ (8).

Top pushed a button. Eight boxing _____ (10) knocked out the octopus. Tip pushed another button. The sub went on sonic power. The octopus _____ (9) them through the water.

Top headed for the _____ (14).

The sub flashed into the _____ (12).

Tip grabbed onto the _____ (16).

Top grabbed onto Tip. It was another close _____ (15).

(Supports Student Book C, pages 58-59) **Completing a crossword puzzle; retelling a story**. Students can refer to student book pages 58–59 to complete the puzzle independently. Check answers in class.

More *Tip Top Adventures*

Complete the "Tip Top Adventure."

1. Tip and Top _____ at a new planet.

2. It was covered by _____ and _____.

3. Tip and Top dressed in their _____ suits.

4. They slid down the ladder and put on their space _____.

5. Icicles froze on Top's_____.

6. Tip discovered huge _____ in the snow.

7. They followed the footprints to a big _____ of snow.

8. Suddenly the snow _____!

9. The giant _____ roared.

10. Tip and Top headed for the _____.

11. Top slipped and fell off his skis. He _____ onto Tip's back.

12. They reached the ladder just in time. Top_____ the hatch shut.
   They blasted off!

(Supports Student Book C, pages 60-61) **Reading for a purpose; cloze story.** Students complete the page independently. Check answers in class.

53

More *Tip Top Adventures*

Write and illustrate a "Tip Top Adventure" of your own.

(Supports Student Book C, pages 58-61) **Creative writing.** Students can work independently or with a partner. Volunteers can share their stories with the class. You may want to save this page in the student's **Assessment Portfolio**.

Mae Jemison, Astronaut

Use the words in the Data Bank. Finish the paragraphs about "Mae Jemison, Astronaut."

Imagine growing up with a dream—a dream to be an _____. Mae

Jemison had that dream, and she made _____ come true. As a child

growing up in _____, she would look up at the _____ and

wonder what was up there. She believed she would travel into _____

someday, but she didn't know _____.

One thing that helped her dream come true was _____ a good

_____. Her _____ helped her read _____ the

subjects she was interested in, and her parents encouraged her,

_____. In high school, she studied _____. She spent many

hours in _____ museums. But science wasn't her _____

interest. Mae was also a _____!

DATA BANK

it	about	only
teachers	too	stars
getting	how	space
science	dancer	education
Chicago	astronaut	hard

(Supports Student Book C, page 62) **Reading comprehension; cloze exercise; syntax; visualizing.** Students read sentences from the story they listened to on student page 62. This exercise provides an opportunity for students to review the story and to learn syntax. Correct in class. You may want to save this page in the student's **Assessment Portfolio.**

Make an Amazing Facts game of your own. Use facts from this book and your student book. You can write new facts, too. Write the correct answers on a separate piece of paper. Ask your teacher to check your game before you exchange games and play with friends.

(Supports Student Book C, page 64) **Creating a game; reading and writing; socializing.** Some students may need help. Encourage students to research answers they don't know. Store games in a box students can access during free time.

Quick Writes

A. *Write down the names of all the states you know.*

_____

_____

_____

_____

_____

B. *Write down the names of all the state capitals you know.*

_____

_____

_____

_____

_____

_____

(Supports Student Book C, page 65) **Using background knowledge related to theme.** After discussing theme opener page 65 in the student book, students list the states and capitals they know. Students can work independently or with a partner. Have them compare their lists. You may want to save this page in the student's **Assessment Portfolio**.

A Interview five friends about where they are from and where they live.

Person Interviewed	Born In	Address	Phone Number
1.			
2.			
3.			
4.			
5.			

Write the questions for these answers.

1. _____

I was born in San Juan.

2. _____

It's in Puerto Rico.

3. _____

When I was eight.

4. _____

It's 583 Addison Street.

5. _____

It's 549-8734.

(Supports Student Book C, page 66) **Data collection; interviewing; asking for and recording information.**
Students use completed charts in the first exercise as springboards for more paired conversations to practice.
Correct the second exercise in class. You may want to save this page in the student's **Assessment Portfolio.**

B *Find the states with the numbers. Write their names on the lines. The first one is done for you.*

1. <u>California</u>

2. _____

3. _____

4. _____

5. _____

6. _____

7. _____

8. _____

9. _____

(Supports Student Book C, page 67) **Reading a map; learning state names.** Students can work independently or with a partner.

More About Magnets

Read the paragraphs and answer the questions.

We use magnets in all kinds of machines. You can find magnets inside refrigerator doors and telephones. Magnets are also in electric motors, food mixers, and drills.

Every magnet has a north pole and a south pole. Two north poles or two south poles push each other apart. We say that two poles of the same kind **repel** each other. That means they push away from each other.

One north pole and one south pole pull each other together. We say that different poles **attract** each other. That means they pull together.

1. Where can you find magnets?

_____

2. How many poles do magnets have?

_____

3. What happens if you try to put two north poles together?

_____

4. What happens if you try to put two south poles together?

_____

5. What happens if you try to put a north pole and a south pole together?

_____

(Supports Student Book C, page 68) **Reading for a purpose; writing.** If necessary, preview the words *repel* and *attract*. Students complete the page independently. Check answers in class. You may want to save this page in the student's **Assessment Portfolio.**

This Land Is Your Land

Write a song and illustrate it.

This _____ is your _____ .

This _____ is my _____ .

From _____ to the _____ .

From the _____   _____ .

To the _____   _____ .

This _____ was made for you and me.

(Supports Student Book C, page 69) **Rewriting a song; learning language through song.** After students have enjoyed "This Land Is Your Land," point out that you can change key words and make a new song about your town, your classroom, or your school. Students work with a partner to make the substitutions. Volunteers can share their new songs with the class.

A *Complete the sentences.*

1. She's a _____

   She _____ sick people.

2. He's a _____ .

   He _____ food.

3. He's a _____

   He _____ a truck.

4. She's a _____ .

   She _____ corn.

5. He's a _____ .

   He _____ the mail.

Answer the questions.

1. Is he a truck driver?

_____

2. Is she a dancer?

_____

3. Is he a farmer?

_____

(Supports Student Book C, page 70) **Matching written language to pictures; describing habitual actions/simple present; affirmative and negative.** Students write the answers to questions on the lines provided. Check in class. You may want to save this page in the student's **Assessment Portfolio**.

B *Use the pictures to answer the questions.*

1. What does he cook?

He cooks chicken.

2. What does he grow?

_____

3. What does he write?

_____

4. What does he play after work?

_____

5. Does she drive a bus?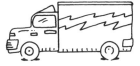

_____

6. Does he grow bananas?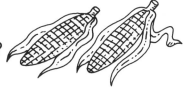

_____

(Supports Student Book C, page 71) **Present tense, third person** *does*; **talking about occupations; matching written language to pictures.** Students complete the page independently. They can practice the dialogues with a partner.

Houses

There are houses
Made of wood,
And houses made of sticks;
There are houses
Made of mud,
And houses made of bricks.

There are houses
That are high,
And houses that are low;
There are houses
that are single,
And houses in a row.

There are houses
In the east,
And houses in the west;
There are houses
All around me—
But my house is the best!

Sophie Tyler

A. *Write a new poem.*

There are _____

Made of _____

And _____ made of _____.

There are _____

That are _____

But my _____ is the _____.

(Supports Student Book C, page 72) **Rewriting a poem; prewriting; learning language through poems.**
After students have heard and read "Houses," they will be aware of its rhymes and rhythms. Students can
point out which lines rhyme. Brainstorm ideas for the new verse they will create by substituting a new subject, such as *clothes* (*shoes, shirt, dress,* or *jacket*).

B. *Finish the sentences.*

The name of a pen pal program is _____. Gary King is a

professional _____ _____ . He is from the state of

_____ . He is also the pen pal of a fourth grade class in

_____ _____ , Wisconsin.

The truckers send _____, _____, and

_____. They send them from all over the _____.

C. *Write a postcard from a place in the United States. Address the
card to your best friend.*

Dear _____,

   Here I am in _____.

It is near _____. There

are many things to do here. You can

_____

_____

_____

_____ .

POSTCARD

Old Glory

USA
Postcard
Rate

_____

_____

_____

_____

(Supports Student Book C, page 73) **Reading for a purpose; writing a postcard.** Students can refer to student book page 73 to complete Exercise B. For Exercise C, encourage them to write about a place they have been, or help them find out about a place they would like to visit. Volunteers can share their postcards with the class. You may want to save this page in the student's **Assessment Portfolio**.

A Write the correct form of each verb.

Miles never (miss) _____ a Little League practice game. After

school, he (rush) _____ home and (brush) _____ his hair

and (wash) _____ his face. He takes out his uniform and (dress)

_____ quickly. Then he (dash) _____ off to the park. He

(chase) _____ baseballs for two hours. He usually (catch)

_____ all the balls he goes after. Miles loves baseball. He (wish)

_____ he could play every day.

*Read each sentence. Write **Yes** if it matches the picture. Write **No** if
it doesn't match the picture. Then write a new sentence.*

1. Maria gets up at 6:00. _____

_____

2. She washes her face. _____

_____

3. She dashes down the street. _____

_____

(Supports Student Book C, page 74) **Describing present actions using simple present tense.** Students work
independently to supply the correct verb forms in first exercise and to supply correct information in the second exercise. You may want to save this page in the student's **Assessment Portfolio.**

Use the words in the Data Bank to complete the puzzle.

DATA BANK

help	washes
delivers	grows
drive	cooks
stamp	dress
	writes

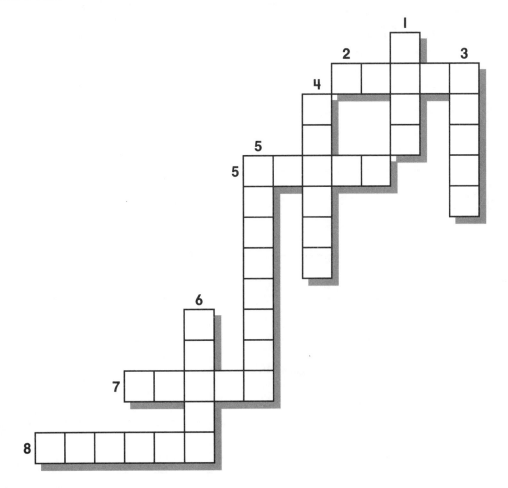

Across

2. They _____ in their baseball uniforms.

5. They _____ a truck.

7. He _____ flowers.

8. She _____ her face.

Down

1. Doctors _____ sick people.

3. They _____ postcards.

4. She _____ books.

5. He _____ the mail.

6. He _____ fish.

(Supports Student Book C, page 75) **Describing habitual actions; completing a crossword puzzle.** Students read the sentences, complete them with verbs that make sense, and write the verb in the correct space.

67

Find out more about the Chippewa people.

1. Where did they first live?

_____

2. Which states make up that land now?

_____

3. Were they peaceful or warlike people?

_____

4. Did they hunt or farm?

_____

5. When did they leave their homelands? Why did that happen?

_____

6. Where do most Chippewa live today?

_____

7. Pretend you are a Chippewa child. What is your life like?

_____

_____

_____

_____

(Supports Student Book C, pages 76-77) **Research; writing; appreciating a different culture.** Students can work with a partner to answer the questions. If necessary, help students find appropriate research materials.

HANDS-ON SOCIAL STUDIES

The Chippewa believe that dream catchers catch bad dreams. They disappear in the web. The good dreams float through the dream catcher web. They travel down the feather and appear in your mind or memory.

A. *Write about a bad dream.*

_____

_____

_____

_____

_____

_____

B. *Write about a good dream.*

_____

_____

_____

_____

_____

_____

(Supports Student Book C, pages 76-77) **Creative writing; appreciating multicultural diversity.** Students record a bad dream and a good dream they had. Encourage them to write as much detail as they can remember. If they can't remember a dream, tell them to make one up.

My Home

Complete the sentences.

I used to live in Agua Calientes, _____. When I was five, my whole

_____ came here, over the hills, across the _____.

We first lived in a _____ with two rooms. Then we moved to this

house. They are both _____ than my house in Mexico. That house was

_____ and it had two floors. Our house here is one room with a

_____. I like the house in Mexico better because it had _____.

Now I sleep with my brother Juan and my _____ in one bed. My

_____ and my sisters Bertha, Fatima, Christina, and Carla sleep in the

other one.

My parents work hard in the _____, _____, _____,

and _____. Juan and Fatima go also, but Bertha stays home to

_____ my little sisters. We help my parents in the _____. I like

to arrange the strawberries in the _____ after I pick them.

I'd like to have a _____ house with gardens in back. I'd like that

when I get _____.

(Supports Student Book C, pages 78-81) **Cloze exercise; retelling a story in sequence; vocabulary development; reading for a purpose.** After students complete the page independently, they can work with a partner: one reads the sentences aloud and the other fills in the missing words. Encourage the students to finish telling the story orally.

My Home

Answer the questions.

1. Where did the Araiza family used to live?

_____

2. How old was Manual when his family came across the border?

_____

3. Where did they live before they moved into their house?

_____

4. What color was their house in Mexico?

_____

5. Why did Manual like the house in Mexico better?

_____

6. Who does Manual sleep with?

_____

7. What fields do Manual's parents work in?

_____

8. Who stays home to watch Manual's little sisters?

_____

9. What does Manual like to do to help his parents?

_____

(Supports Student Book C, pages 78–81) **Recalling details; drawing conclusions; reading comprehension.**
Students complete the page independently. Help them think of questions and answers that finish telling the
story. You may want to save this page in the student's **Assessment Portfolio**.

My Home

Draw a bigger house for the Araiza family to live in. Then write a description of the house and tell where each person in the family will sleep.

_____

_____

_____

_____

_____

_____

_____

(Supports Student Book C, pages 78-81) **Describing a drawing; art.** Students work independently to complete the page. Volunteers can read their descriptions aloud.

My Home

Draw your own dream house that you would like to live in when you're older. Then write a description of the house.

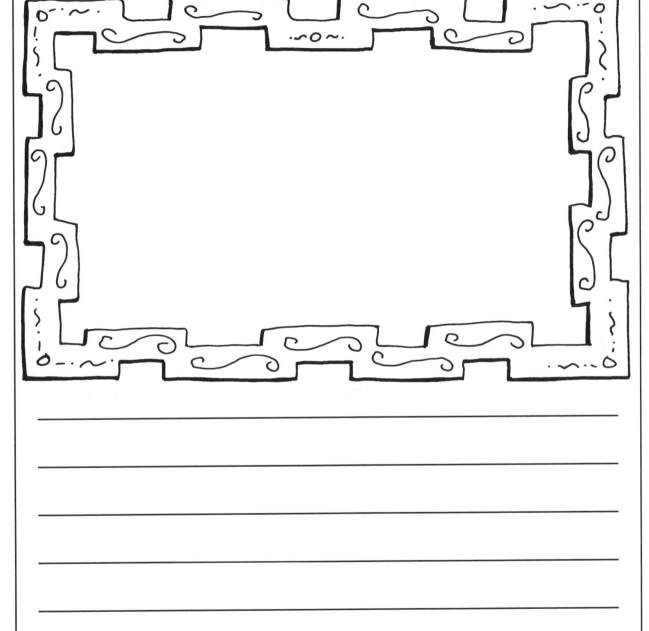

_____

_____

_____

_____

_____

_____

_____

(Supports Student Book C, pages 78-81) **Home-School Connection; describing a drawing; art.** Students work independently to complete the page. You may want to help students brainstorm ideas for their dream house. Volunteers can read their descriptions aloud. Display the drawings on a bulletin board. You may want to save a copy of this page in the student's **Assessment Portfolio**. Have students take this page home to share with their families.

The Amazing Anasazi

Use the words in the Data Bank. Finish the paragraphs about "The Amazing Anasazi."

The Anasazi Indians lived _____ ago in the _____. Look at

a _____. Find the place where New Mexico, _____, Arizona,

and Utah meet. Then find _____ _____, Colorado. Now listen

and try to _____ what _____ was like for the Anasazi people

there in the year 1250.

The Anasazi lived in an amazing kind of "apartment house." They

_____ this house on the _____ of a steep _____. The

mountain rose more than 700 feet in the air. That's _____ how tall a

70-story _____ is! In this amazing _____ house, there were

more _____ 200 rooms, or _____.

DATA BANK

map	building	Colorado
apartments	cliff	long
imagine	side	than
life	Mesa Verde	built
Southwest	mountain	about

(Supports Student Book C, page 82) **Reading comprehension; cloze exercise; syntax.** Students read sentences from the story they listened to on student page 82. This exercise provides an opportunity for students to review the story and to learn syntax. Correct in class. You may want to save this page in the student's **Assessment Portfolio.**

74

Make an Amazing Facts game of your own. Use facts from this book and your student book. You can write new facts, too. Write the correct answers on a separate piece of paper. Ask your teacher to check your game before you exchange games and play with friends.

(Supports Student Book C, page 84) **Creating a game; reading and writing; socializing.** Some students may need help. Encourage students to research answers they don't know. Store games in a box students can access during free time.

Quick Writes

A. *Work with your student book open to page 85. Describe the photo. Then tell what you think the story about the gorilla will be about.*

_____

_____

_____

_____

B. *Write about a wild animal that you like.*

_____

_____

_____

C. *Write about a tame animal that you like.*

_____

_____

_____

(Supports Student Book C, page 85) **Writing about a photo; predicting.** After discussing theme opener page 85 in the student book, students write a description of the photo and what they think the Koko story will be about. For Exercises B and C, you may want to discuss the difference between *wild* and *tame*. Encourage students to share what they write. You may want to save this page in the student's **Assessment Portfolio**.

Interview five friends about their favorite animals.

Person Interviewed	Favorite Wild Animal	Favorite Pet	Favorite Animal Movie
1.			
2.			
3.			
4.			
5.			

Write the questions to these answers.

1. _____

   I like giraffes.

2. _____

   My favorite pet is a dog.

3. _____

   Her name is Sparky.

4. _____

   I like *The Lion King*.

(Supports Student Book C, page 86) **Data collection; interviewing; asking for and recording information.**
Students use completed charts in the first exercise as springboards for more paired conversations to practice
Correct the second exercise in class. You may want to save this page in the student's **Assessment Portfolio.**

Complete the story with words in the Data Bank.

DATA BANK

fix	watch
look	cross
walk	rush
kiss	

Last Saturday, I _____ out of my house to go play soccer in the

park. Mom _____ me good-bye. As I _____ the bridge near

the park, I _____ over at the other side of the road. A little boy had a

broken skate. His mother _____ it for him. I _____ them. Then

the little boy and his mother _____ toward the park.

(Supports Student Book C, page 87) **Describing past actions.** Tell students to make the verbs in the Data Bank past tense. Have them work independently to complete this page.

Money

Read the paragraphs and answer the questions.

Before 1901, coins in the United States did not have a picture of anybody's head on them. Many coins had an eagle or the symbol of Liberty. But in 1909, 100 years after Lincoln was born, the Lincoln penny appeared. This coin had the head of Abraham Lincoln on one side and Liberty on the other side.

George Washington's head did not appear on a coin until 200 years after he was born. His head is on the quarter, 25 cents.

President Roosevelt's head appeared on the dime, 10 cents, in 1946. In 1964, the Kennedy half dollar, 50 cents, appeared, less than a year after the president's death.

The Eisenhower silver dollar appeared in 1970, just ten years after Eisenhower left office.

1. When did the first pictures of people's heads appear on United States coins?

_____

2. When was Lincoln born?

_____

3. What coin is Washington's head on?

_____

4. What happened in 1946?

_____

5. When did Kennedy's head appear on a coin?

_____

(Supports Student Book C, page 88) **Reading for a purpose; writing.** Students complete the page independently. Check answers in class.

Do the Dog Walk

Write new verses for "Do the Dog Walk." Teach your song to your friends. Then everybody can sing all the new verses for other classes!

When I was a little _____,
I'd play and play and play;

Now I am a big _____,
And this is what I say.

_____, _____ — do the _____ talk!

_____, _____ — do the _____ walk!

When I was a little _____ ,
I'd play and play and play;

Now I am a big _____ ,
And this is what I say.

_____, _____ — do the _____ talk!

_____, _____ — do the _____ walk!

When I was a little _____,
I'd play and play and play;

Now I am a big _____,
And this is what I say.

_____, _____ — do the _____ talk!

_____, _____ —do the _____ walk!

(Supports Student Book C, page 89) **Writing new poetry verses.** Students can complete the page independently or with a partner. Volunteers can teach their new verses to the class. Then the class can sing them for other classes. You may want to save this page in the student's **Assessment Portfolio**.

COMMUNICATION 2

A *Look at the pictures.
Answer each question.*

*Tell a story. Use the pictures to
answer the questions.*

1. Did she climb on a table?

No, she didn't. She climbed on the ladder.

1. Where did Raoul live?

_____

_____

2. Did she open the door?

_____

2. What did he dream about?

_____

3. Did they move to Texas?

_____

_____

3. Where did he play?

_____

_____

(Supports Student Book C, page 90) **Matching written language to pictures.** Students work with a partner
to write the answers to the questions. Then volunteers share their answers with the class.

B *Write answers to the questions.*

1. What did she check out?  _____

2. What did she listen to? _____

3. What did she look at? _____

4. What did she borrow? _____

Interview a friend.

Name _____

1. What are you interested in?

_____

_____

2. What kind of books do you like?

_____

_____

3. What kind of music do you listen to?

_____

_____

4. What do you like to do?

_____

_____

(Supports Student Book C, page 91) **Asking/answering questions; interviewing.** Students work independently to complete the first exercise and in pairs to complete the second exercise. You may want to save this page in the student's **Assessment Portfolio.**

Check This Out!

More About Bugs

Read the paragraphs and answer the questions.

All insects' bodies are made up of three sections: the head, the thorax, and the abdomen. Eyes and antennas are attached to the head. The wings and legs—if the insect has any—are attached to the thorax.

Many common insects change their forms completely in their lives. A butterfly, for example, looks very different from its parents when it hatches from an egg as a larva. It also eats very different food. When it is full-grown, it becomes a pupa and changes into an adult butterfly.

1. How many sections does an insect's body have?

_____

2. Where are an insect's legs attached?

_____

3. Where do baby insects come from?

_____

4. What is the insect called when it changes from a larva to an adult?

_____

5. Do all insects have wings and legs?

_____

(Supports Student Book C, page 92) **Reading for a purpose; writing.** Students complete the page independently. Check answers in class. You may want to save this page in the student's **Assessment Portfolio**.

83

Write and illustrate some new short poems of your own.

Way Down South

Way down south where _____ grow,

A _____ stepped on a _____ toe.

The _____ said, with tears in his eyes,
"Pick on somebody your own size."

Way Up North

Way up north where _____ grow,

A _____ stepped on a _____ toe.

The _____ said, with tears in his eyes,
"Pick on somebody your own size."

Way Out West

Way out west where _____ grow,

A _____ stepped on a _____ toe.

The _____ said, with tears in his eyes,
"Pick on somebody your own size."

_____
(Title)

_____

_____

_____

(Supports Student Book C, page 92) **Writing new poetry verses.** Students can complete the page independently or with a partner. Volunteers can read their poems aloud.

LANGUAGE POWER

A *Complete the puzzle.*

DATA BANK

paint	collect
lift	play
want	count
plant	

Across

2. I **played** my guitar.

3. She _____ a new camera.

4. I _____ my desk.

5. She _____ her money.

6. We _____ the heavy box.

Down

1. Grandpa _____ stamps.

4. He _____ a tree.

(Supports Student Book C, page 94) **Writing past tense verbs; completing a crossword puzzle.** Students fill in the blanks with the past tense of verbs in the Data Bank and write them in the crossword puzzle.

85

B Complete the conversation with these words.

DATA BANK

my	our	this	these
your	their	that	those
his, her, its			

★ I lost _____ socks. Can I wear _____ socks?

● What do you mean? I need _____ socks. Look! Here are

_____ socks under _____ bed.

★ Oh, yeah! Look! The dog put _____ bone inside _____ sock

over there.

● You and the dog were both looking for _____ socks!

(Supports Student Book C, page 95) **Expressing ownership.** Students work independently to complete the cloze exercise. Then they share their responses with the class. Follow up: Students work with a partner or in groups to create their own humorous conversations.

HANDS-ON **S**CIENCE

Elephant Facts

Read the paragraphs and answer the questions.

An elephant's head weighs about one quarter of the animal's total weight. Its tusks are its front teeth.

An elephant can smell and taste with its trunk. It can also squirt water and dust. But the trunk is very strong and sensitive. It can lift trees or pick up pebbles.

Elephants can live for 70 years. A mother elephant carries its babies for 22 months before the babies are born.

An adult elephant eats about 300 pounds of grass, leaves, and twigs every day!

1. If an elephant weighs 16,000 pounds, how heavy is its head?

_____

2. How many years can some elephants live?

_____

3. How long are baby elephants carried inside their mother?

_____

4. How much does an elephant eat every day?

_____

5. Name some things an elephant can do with its trunk.

_____

(Supports Student Book C, pages 96-97) **Reading for a purpose; writing.** Students complete the page independently. Check answers in class.

87

Koko

Read and think carefully. Then complete the sentences. Check your answers with pages 98–101 in your student book.

1. Koko the gorilla was born in a _____.

2. When she was very young, she moved to the state of _____.

3. Dr. Patterson is Koko's trainer and _____.

4. Dr. Patterson taught Koko ASL— _____ _____

_____.

5. Koko learned more than _____ words in ASL.

6. When Koko was a baby, her favorite story was _____

_____ _____ _____.

7. Now Koko is all grown up and has her own _____.

8. Koko plays _____ and answers _____.

9. Koko likes to _____, _____, and _____ in

her yard.

10. Her favorite foods are _____, _____, and

_____.

(Supports Student Book C, pages 98-101) **Reading for a purpose; completing a cloze exercise.** Students complete the page independently. Check answers in class. You may want to save this page in the student's **Assessment Portfolio.**

Koko

Use the American Sign Language alphabet on page 90 to do these exercises.

A. *What do these signs say?*

_____   _____ _____

_____   _____

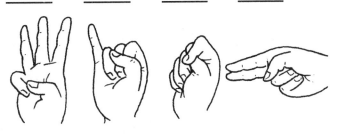

_____

_____ _____   _____ _____ _____

B. *Make up your own message from the symbols and sign it to your friends.*

(Supports Student Book C, pages 98-101) **Communicating through American Sign Language; socializing.**
Students complete Exercise A independently. Check answers in class. For Exercise B, students work with a partner to write messages and sign them to each other. Give students time to practice the signs.

ASL Alphabet

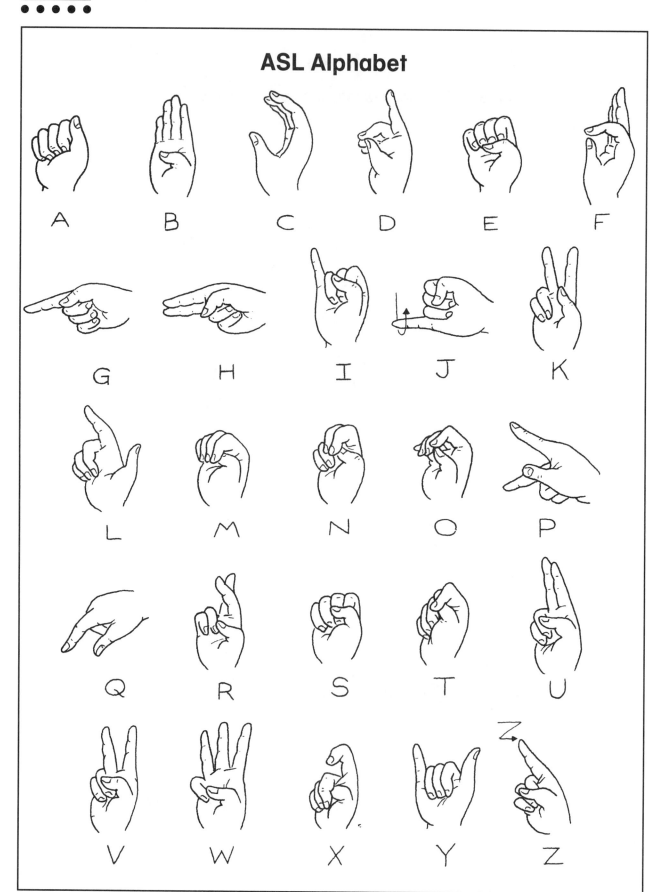

The King of the Beasts

Use the words in the Data Bank. Finish the paragraphs about "The King of the Beasts."

Lions, like _____, live in family groups. A group of lions is called a

_____. A pride can be quite _____ or quite large. It can

have as few as _____ lions or as many as forty. One full-grown

_____ is the head of the pride. But he doesn't really do much. All the

_____ is done by the _____. They hunt alone and in

_____.

A lion can run very _____ for a short period of time. It can reach

_____ of 60 to 70 miles an hour. A lion is also a good

_____. It can _____ 40 feet in a single bound. Lions are the

only _____ of the _____ family that _____.

DATA BANK

leap	speeds	pride
females	members	teams
cat	gorillas	roar
small	fast	hunting
male	four	jumper

(Supports Student Book C, page 102) **Reading comprehension; cloze exercise; syntax.** Students read sentences from the story they listened to on student page 102. This exercise provides an opportunity for students to review the story and to learn syntax. Correct in class. You may want to save this page in the student's **Assessment Portfolio.**

Make an Amazing Facts game of your own. Use facts from this book and your student book. You can write new facts, too. Write the correct answers on a separate piece of paper. Ask your teacher to check your game before you exchange games and play with friends.

(Supports Student Book C, page 104) **Creating a game; reading and writing; socializing.** Some students may need help. Encourage students to research answers they don't know. Store games in a box students can access during free time.

Quick Writes

A. *Describe the photograph on page 105 of your student book.*

_____

_____

_____

_____

B. *Draw a picture of your favorite season. Write about what you like to do then.*

_____

_____

_____

(Supports Student Book C, page 105) **Writing about a photograph; expressing ideas through art.** After discussing theme opener page 105 in the student book, students write a description of the photograph. You may want to save this page in the student's **Assessment Portfolio.**

A Interview five friends. Fill in the chart. Compare your chart with your classmates' charts.

Person Interviewed	Favorite season	Favorite activity
1.		
2.		
3.		
4.		
5.		

Write questions for these answers.

1. _____

   My favorite season is summer.

2. _____

   I like hot weather.

3. _____

   I go swimming and bike riding.

4. _____

   My favorite season is spring.

5. _____

   I like apple blossoms.

6. _____

   I plant my garden.

(Supports Student Book C, page 106) **Data collection; interviewing; asking for and recording information.** Students use completed charts in the first exercise and questions and answers in the second exercise as springboards for more paired conversations to practice.

B *Mark the things that don't belong in each season picture with a big X.*

Summer

A. _____

_____

Winter

B. _____

_____

© Addison-Wesley Publishing Company

(Supports Student Book C, page 107) **Identifying the seasons and their weather.** Students have fun X-ing out the items that don't belong. Then they share their work with their classmates, for example, *The boy in the snowsuit and boots doesn't belong here.* Help them list items on the lines provided.

High Flyers

Read the paragraphs and answer the questions.

Orville and Wilbur Wright were brothers from Ohio. They published a newspaper. Later, they repaired and sold bicycles. But that is not why we remember them today. The two brothers spent a lot of time watching birds. They studied how they moved their wings when they flew.

On December 14, 1903, Orville and Wilbur tried to take off from Kill Devil Hill in North Carolina in a plane they had built. The plane didn't get off the ground. But three days later, Orville flew the plane for twelve seconds.

On the same day, they made three more flights. The longest was 59 seconds. It was five more years before anyone else kept a plane in the air for more than a minute. And by that time, the Wright brothers were flying for more than an hour at a time!

1. What work did the Wright brothers do?

_____

2. What did they study?

_____

3. When did they fly an airplane for the first time?

_____

4. How many flights did the Wright brothers make the first day?

_____

5. How long was it before other people made longer flights?

_____

(Supports Student Book C, page 108) **Reading for a purpose; writing.** Students complete the page independently. Check answers in class. You may want to save this page in the student's **Assessment Portfolio.**

Dreams

A. *What do you think of when you see this word? Write down the words you think of. The write a paragraph about DREAMS.*

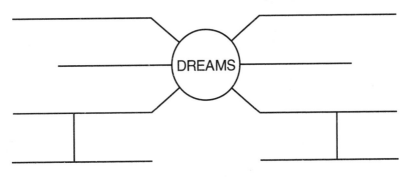

DREAMS

_____

_____

_____

_____

_____

_____

_____

B. *Finish the poem with your own words.*

Hold fast to dreams
For if dreams die

Life is _____

_____.

(Supports Student Book C, page 109) **Brainstorming; finishing a poem.** Use exercise A to brainstorm with students about dreams. Then encourage them to write a paragraph about the subject. In Exercise B, students finish the poem in their own words. Volunteers can share their paragraphs and poems. You may want to save this page in the student's **Assessment Portfolio**.

A Answer the questions in complete sentences.

1. When did he get up? _____

2. What did he eat? _____

3. What did he drink? _____

4. Where did he go? _____

5. What did he ride? _____

6. What did he catch? _____

Answer the questions in complete sentences.

1. When did you get up today?

_____

2. What did you eat for breakfast?

_____

3. What did you drink?

_____

4. What did you ride to school?

_____

5. Where did you go yesterday?

_____

© Addison-Wesley Publishing Company

(Supports Student Book C, page 110) **Telling a story in question and answer form; practicing conversations.** Students work independently to complete the page. Then have them work with a partner to practice conversations in the second exercise. You may want to save this page in the student's **Assessment Portfolio**.

B *Look at the pictures and complete the conversations.*

1. What's the weather like?

    It's _____.

2. What's the weather forecast?

    It's going to be _____.

3. How's the weather?

    It's _____.
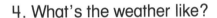

4. What's the weather like?

    It's _____.

Read the sentences and think carefully. Then complete the sentences.

1. It's very hot at the beach. I'll wear my _____.

2. It's rainy today. I'll wear my _____ and _____.

3. It's snowing! I'll wear my _____, _____, and

    _____.

4. It's windy. I think I'll fly a _____.

5. It's so hot. I think I'll drink _____.

6. It's so cold. I think I'll drink _____.

(Supports Student Book C, page 111) **Asking/answering questions; using weather vocabulary; practicing conversations.** If necessary, help students brainstorm appropriate vocabulary for the second exercise. Then have them work with a partner to make practice conversations from the first exercise.

Check This Out!

A. *Find out the highest average temperatures for the cities in the box. Write the names of the cities on lines **a** through **h** below the graph. Write them in order of their temperatures (highest to lowest). Draw a line on the graph at the highest degree for each city. The first one is done for you.*

Salt Lake City, UT	Las Vegas, NV
Madison, WI	Austin, TX
Cincinnati, OH	Washington, D.C.
Atlanta, GA	Omaha, NB

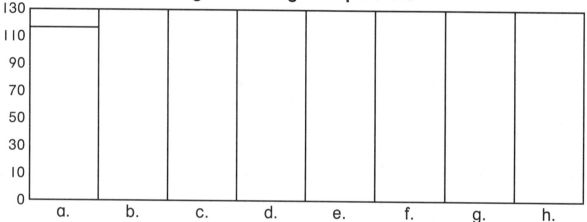

Highest Average Temperature

a. <u>Las Vegas, NV</u>

b. _____

c. _____

d. _____

e. _____

f. _____

g. _____

h. _____

(Supports Student Book C, pages 112-113) **Research; filling in a graph.** You may need to help some students find information about average temperatures. As an extension, students can find out other weather information for one or more of the states in the graph and share it with the class. You may want to save this page in the student's **Assessment Portfolio.**

More About Penguins

B. *Read the paragraphs and answer the questions.*

Penguins live south of the equator in the Southern Hemisphere. Some penguins live on the ice of Antarctica. All penguins are mainly black and white. Some penguins are bigger than others.

The Emperor penguin is the biggest. It is three feet tall. It lays its eggs on the ice at the beginning of the Antarctic winter. The weather is severe. Temperatures are below freezing. Snow and hurricane winds blow across the ice. There is no food.

The male penguins stand over the eggs for 60 days to keep them warm. During this time, they lose half their body weight. After the chicks hatch, only one chick in five survives.

Emperor penguins are good swimmers. They can dive to almost 900 feet below the water. They can stay underwater for nine minutes!

1. Where do penguins live?

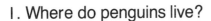

_____

2. Do all penguins look the same?

_____

3. What is the biggest penguin called?

_____

4. Who takes care of the eggs?

_____

5. What can penguins do that you can't do?

_____

A Look at the pictures. Then write sentences that tell what the people have to do. Use **He has to, She has to,** or **They have to.**

1. _____

2. _____

3. _____

4. _____

5. _____

6. _____

What do you have to do at home?

_____

_____

_____

(Supports Student Book C, page 114) **Using** *has to/have to* **in sentences; writing about activities.**
Students complete the page independently. Check answers to the first exercise in class. Volunteers can share their sentences in the second exercise. You may want to save this page in the student's **Assessment Portfolio.**

102

B *What did they have to do yesterday? Use **had to** in complete sentences.*

1. _____

2. _____

3. _____

4. _____

5. _____

6. _____

What did you have to do yesterday? Last Saturday?

_____

_____

_____

(Supports Student Book C, page 115) **Home-School Connection; using *had to* in sentences; writing about activities.** Students complete the page independently. Check the answers to the first exercise in class. Volunteers can share their sentences in the second exercise. Have students take this page home to share with their families.

What's the Weather?

Keep a record of the weather for a week. Fill in the chart every day. The first day is done for you as an example.

	Sun	Clouds	Wind	Rain/ Snow	High Temp.	Comments
Monday	✓		✓			bright sunshine with a light breeze
Tuesday						
Wednesday						
Thursday						
Friday						
Saturday						
Sunday						

(Supports Student Book C, pages 116-117) **Observing weather; data collection; completing a chart.**
Students keep records of the weather for a week by putting checkmarks in the first four columns and writing the high temperature in the fifth column. For the Comments column, encourage students to briefly describe clouds, wind, or precipitation.

The Grateful Statues

Find the correct pictures and number them.

1. The poor woman made straw hats.
2. The man sold the straw hats.
3. It started to snow.
4. The man gave the hats to the statues.
5. The man told the woman about the statues.
6. Outside their door, they found two huge rice cakes.

(Supports Student Book C, pages 118-123) **Understanding details; spelling; matching written language to pictures.** Students do the exercise independently and go over the answers with the class.

The Grateful Statues

A. *Read each sentence. Check **YES** or **NO**.*

	YES	NO
1. The poor man lived alone.	_____	_____
2. The man and his wife lived in a big city.	_____	_____
3. It was the last day of the year.	_____	_____
4. It was summer and the weather was warm.	_____	_____
5. The man gave the sixth statue his own hat.	_____	_____
6. The statues gave the man and his wife new straw hats.	_____	_____

B. *What is the word?*

1. IRCE

_____

2. ONYEM

_____

3. AKCES

_____

4. EUTSTA

_____

5. THA

_____

5. WSON

_____

(Supports Student Book C, pages 118-123) **Understanding details; spelling; matching written language to pictures.** Students do the exercise independently and go over the answers with the class. You may want to save this page in the student's **Assessment Portfolio.**

Why the Sky Is Far Away

Use the words in the Data Bank. Finish the paragraphs about "Why the Sky Is Far Away."

Long ago, the sky was _____ to the _____. Men and

women did not have to _____ their own food. They _____

have to cook. When they _____ hungry, they just reached

_____ and broke off a piece of the sky to eat! Sometimes the sky

tasted like ripe _____. Other times it tasted like roasted

_____. The sky was _____ delicious.

People spent their time making beautiful _____. They painted

beautiful _____ and sang songs at night. The grand king, Oba,

_____ a wonderful palace. His servants made beautiful shapes out of

pieces _____ sky.

Many people in the kingdom did not use the _____ of the sky wisely.

When they took more than they could eat, the sky became_____.

DATA BANK

gift	earth	close
cloth	angry	up
potatoes	bananas	always
plant	didn't	were
pictures	of	had

(Supports Student Book C, page 124) **Reading comprehension; cloze exercise; syntax.** Students read sentences from the story they listened to on page 124. This exercise peovides an opportunity for students to review the story and to learn syntax. correct in class. You may want to save this page in the student's **Assessment Portfolio**.

Make an Amazing Facts game of your own. Use facts from this book and your student book. You can write new facts, too. Write the correct answers on a separate piece of paper. Ask your teacher to check your game before you exchange games and play with friends.

(Supports Student Book C, page 126) **Creating a game; reading and writing; socializing.** Some students may need help. Encourage students to research answers they don't know. Store games in a box students can access during free time.

Read the words and find the picture. Circle the letter under the correct picture.

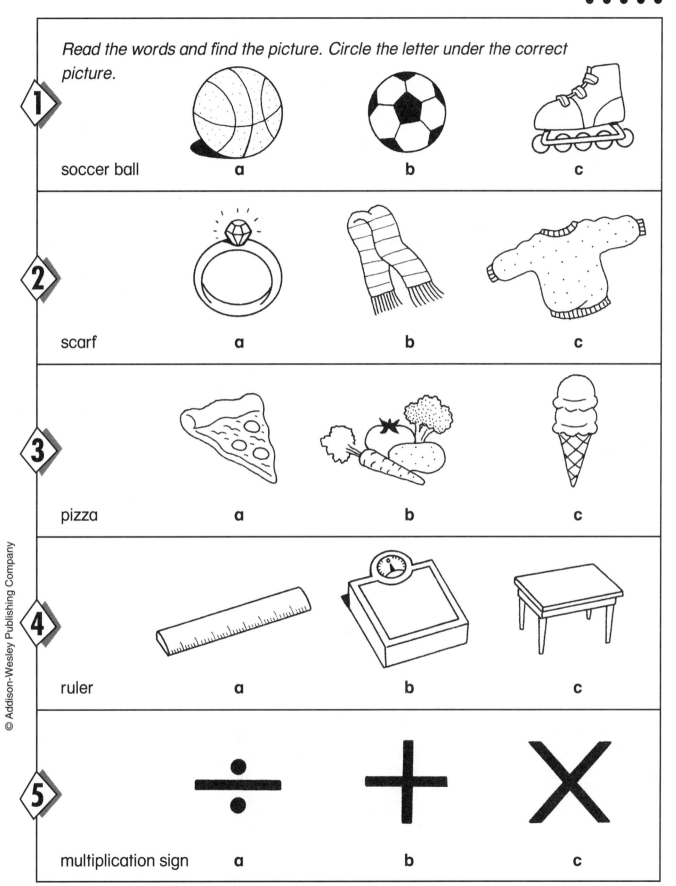

1

soccer ball   **a**   **b**   **c**

2

scarf   **a**   **b**   **c**

3

pizza   **a**   **b**   **c**

4

ruler   **a**   **b**   **c**

5

multiplication sign   **a**   **b**   **c**

(Supports Student Book C) **Preparation for standardized testing: reading.** Students work independently. You may want to save this page in the student's **Assessment Portfolio**.

Find the picture that goes with each sentence. Circle the letter under the correct picture.

1

She's wearing a sweater.   a   b   c

2

They're eating apples.   a   b   c

3

They're wearing sneakers.   a   b   c

4

He's wearing gloves.   a   b   c

5

He's standing next to the chair.   a   b   c

(Supports Student Book C) **Preparation for standardized testing: reading.** Students work independently. You may want to save this page in the student's **Assessment Portfolio**.

Listen and find the picture. Fill in the oval. Color the picture.

(Supports Student Book C) **Preparation for standardized testing: listening.** After doing the first item together, students do the four items independently, marking the oval under the correct illustrations, and the coloring as directed. (Script in Teacher's Guide Appendix) You may want to save this page in the student's **Assessment Portfolio.**